BISHOPS

EXTRAORDINARY

by

KARL PRUTER

St. Willibrord Press

1985

Highlandville, MO

Table of Contents

THE AUTOCEPHALOUS MOVEMENT

and

BISHOPS EXTRAORDINARY

Two events moved me to write about the five extraordinary bishops of the autocephalous movement. First, this year marks the 100th anniversary of the ordination of Joseph Rene Vilatte. Second, the publication of the "Directory of the Autocephalous Bishops" graphically shows the number, the variety, and the diversity of Christian jurisdictions that have been spawned by Bishops Mathew, de Landes Berghes, Vilatte, Carfora and Ofiesh.

I must confess to one more motivation. All five of these men have been written about by such men as Peter Anson, H. R. T. Brandreth, and C. B. Moss. Each of these authors managed to vilify the bishops by repeating slanders but more often by a lack of sympathy and a failure to understand the odds against which these bishops struggled. We need to examine, very briefly, what it is that these men had in common, the cause for which they fought and struggled and what made them "Bishops Extraordinary."

Starting arbitrarily with Arbishop Arnold Harris Mathew we see a man who desires to be "Catholic" but who finds that his native land offers only two choices. Although he began his ministry as a Roman priest in July of 1877 he informed his parishoners a

decade later that he doubted the
doctrine of Papal infallibility.   The
next few years he attempted to find out
where he belonged.   He briefly served
the Unitarians and then went to the
Anglican Church.   The Anglican Church,
was, and still is, a Church divided by
protestant and catholic factions.   Its
orders are not recognized by the Roman
Church and the doctrine of Holy Orders
is not believed by much of its membership, including priests and bishops.
Not for long could Arnold Harris
Mathew feel comfortable in a church that
was neither Protestant or Catholic but
a hybrid.

He, like Joseph Rene Vilatte in
America, looked to Utrecht.   The
ancient See of Utrecht had been separated from Rome since the latter part
of the seventeenth century and its
orders and faith were catholic.   More
importantly, to Mathew and Vilatte was
the fact that, although separated from
Rome, Rome by its own doctrinal stand-
ards, had to recognize the Orders and
the Mass of the Church of Utrecht as
valid.   Nor was it an insignificant
diocese, for in Hollard alone, there
were 30,000 catholics who claimed
Utrecht as their spiritual home.   Since,
Vatican I, which was held in 1870, many
more thousands of European Catholics
left Rome for Utrecht over the question
of Papal infallibility.   Catholics in
Southern Germany, Switzerland, and
Austria separated from Rome and formed
national Old Catholic Churches.   These
Churches formed a Union with Utrecht and
the bishops they elected for their

national groups were consecrated by the bishops of Utrecht, Deventer and Haarlam and thus valid in the eyes of Rome.

Mathew reasoned, as did Vilatte, that if he were to receive orders from Utrecht, he would be able to build a viable Catholic Church in his native country that would be more acceptable to his countrymen than either the Roman Church, whose pontiff claimed infallibility, or the Anglican Church which, perhaps, because it was fallible couldn't decide whether it was Catholic or not. The idea did have wide appeal, but the existing churches, particularly the Anglican Church, attempted to thwart the efforts of these two men. Attacks were often personal and had nothing to do with doctrine. It is very interesting that the size of their following, their personal poverty, and their lack of impressive buildings were frequently cited in an effort to discredit them. Obviously these same critics would have had difficulty with the small and equally poor group that Christ left to carry on His work.

Both Arnold Mathew and Prince de Landas Berghes found that as minor royalty they were often invited to Anglican social gatherings but seldom as bishops, poor and "unrecognized". What was true for these men was also true for Carmel Henry Carfora and Joseph Vilatte. They were measured by the number of followers, the size of the buildings which housed their congregations, and the wealth or lack of wealth of their bishops. If they had become wealthy it is easy to

imagine what form the criticism would
have taken.

Only the story of Aftimios Ofiesh
differs in some small degree. He began
with the recognition and the support of
Metropolitan Platon of the Russian
Orthodox Church. He already served the
Church as Archbishop and the vision
which he had of a united Orthodox Church
in America was shared by his superiors.
He only began to share a common lot with
the other four extraordinary bishops
when the Church which gave him his
apostolate lost faith in that vision.
In the early part of the twentieth
century the various ethnic Orthodox
jurisdictions were not ready to drop
their differences and form an American
Orthodox Church. But the task which
seemed too difficult for the power and
the wealth of the Russian Orthodox
Church was taken on by a simple Lebanese,
named Aftimios Ofiesh. He had accepted
the challenge when it was given to him
by Metropolitan Platon and he would
continue to carry on his apostolate for
the remainder of his life. He too,
would be poor, have few followers, and
build very few and very modest church
buildings. What he did accomplish was
to challenge every Orthodox jurisdiction
in America to the need for English as
the liturgical language and to work for
the Americanization of the Orthodox
Church. English has made some inroads
and while there is little Americanization
the challenge refuses to go away.

Each of the five bishops has given
America, one hundred years after

Vilatte's ordination, many small
Churches determined to build Orthodox
and Catholic jurisdictions free from
infallible popes and bishops, and
independent of any particular ethnic
heritage. They are remembered not only
for their vision but also for their
courage in pursuing their vision in the
face of insurmountable obstacles and
opposition. They had many failures, a
few successes, and indefatigable courage.
They were Bishops Extraordinary!

ARNOLD HARRIS MATHEW

1852 - 1919

Arnold Harris Mathew was born of English parents on August 6, 1852 in France. His father, the third Earl of Landaff, was a Roman Catholic and his mother was a member of the Church of England. As a result, he was baptized with Catholic rites in France and two years later he was conditionally re-baptized by an Anglican clergyman. As he grew up he would attend the Roman Church for a while and then he would attend an Anglican Church and he said that he could hardly see any difference between them.

In 1874 he felt a call to the Anglican ministry and began his training at the College of the Holy Spirit, which was located on the Island of Greater Cumbrae. The Anglican Church which served the college was definitely not "high" church and, perhaps, for this reason Arnold Mathew found himself in an uncongenial environment. He sought admission to the Roman Church and requested that he be permitted to continue his study for Holy Orders, but this time, in

the "true" church. Curiously, he was given
a second conditional baptism. In January
1876 he was admitted to St. Peter's Seminary
at Partickhill, Glasgow. He took a crash
program and in about eighteen months, he was
awarded the degree of Doctor of Divinity.
He was ordained to the Roman Catholic
priesthood on June 24, 1877 by Archbishop
Charles Eyre of Anazarba. A short time
later, he received the degree of Doctor of
Divinity from Pope Pius IX and served in a
number of English parishes until 1898 when
he announced to his congregation that he
doubted the doctrine of Papal Infallibility.

He retired from the active ministry and
assumed the title which was his de jure,
as the fourth Earl of Landaff. The title,
while legitimate, brought no land or per-
quisites with it. Perhaps, this is significant because Mathew in his lifetime consecrated bishops who were to have no laity
to serve, no property to administer, and
often no church or chapel in which to celebrate Mass. The Anglican Church, which he
left to become a Roman priest, was not particularly anxious to reinstate him. He was
permitted to perform some services at the
Church of the Holy Trinity in Westminster.
It was a fashionable Church and the parishoners seemed to respond as much to his
title, the Earl of Landaff, as to his
preaching. While serving at Holy Trinity
he married Margaret Duncan and thereby cut
himself off, forever, from the Roman priesthood. He also gave up his clerical duties
at the Church of the Holy Trinity and tried
his hand at writing. He was quite successful and among his literary works was a
translation of Monsignor Duchesne's, "The
Churches Separated from Rome."

The work appeared in 1907 and in this same year Mathew met Father Richard O'Halloran, who was responsible for introducing him to a new option. Father O'Halloran was a dissatisfied Roman Catholic priest and he and a few fellow pastors were interested in the Old Catholic Movement in Holland. They conceived the idea of an Old Catholic Church of Great Britain that would be catholic and independent of Rome. Surely, Father O'Halloran reasoned with Mathew, this is what he too, had been searching for. For Father Mathew had told his Roman Catholic congregation that he could not accept the doctrine of Papal Infallibility, and yet, he could not accept Anglican teachings as expressed in the 39 Articles. The facts were plain, that Arnold Harris Mathew, not only belonged in the Old Catholic Church, but he would be the ideal head of a British Old Catholic Church, if one could be organized. Fr. O'Halloran assured the Earl of Landaff that seventeen priests and sixteen laymen had elected him to be the first bishop of the Old Catholic movement in England. Arnold Harris Mathew never doubted that there had been an election and that the numbers which Fr. O'Halloran gave him were correct. He refused to accept and it was only after much discussion over a period of weeks that Fr. O'Halloran persuaded him.

From this point on Fr. Richard O'Halloran remained quietly in the background and allowed the new bishop-

elect to contact the Old Catholics in
Europe regarding his consecration. He
began by writing to Bishop Edward Herzog,
the Christ Catholic bishop of
Switzerland. Later he would contact
Bishop Van Thiel of Haarlem. Most of
the correspondence concerned whether
there were or were not, people in England
who desired an Old Catholic Church.
Bishop Herzog stated at the outset, that
the Old Catholic Church did not wish to
consecrate a bishop "in partibus" but
Mathew continued to assure him that in
addition to those who elected him, there
were thousands of dissatisfied Anglicans
who would join a British Old Catholic
Church if it were offered. First, there
were the Modernists, who wanted to be
Catholics, but who could not adapt to the
rigid Roman theology. Second, there were
those who feared the report of the Ritual
Commission which was set up in 1904 to
ferret out illegal rituals and practices
in the Church of England. These feared
that the state would not allow them to be
as Catholic as they wished to be and if
they happened to be married priests they
would not be welcome as priests by the
Roman Church. All this seemed quite
reasonable and besides, didn't the
bishop-elect have a small but solid
nucleus? After all seventeen priests
who were willing to lay their careers on
the line was impressive.

The European Old Catholics never
checked to see if, indeed, there had
been an election and whether the electors
truly existed. They also neglected to
ask the Earl of Landaff, if there was a

Lady Landaff. The Old Catholics of
Europe, like their Orthdox counterparts,
did not permit married bishops. However,
news of his marriage reached Bishop
Herzog and he promptly informed the
Dutch bishops about it. They were dis-
turbed, but for reasons not known, they
decided to go ahead with the consecration
and on April 28, 1908 Archbishop Gul,
assisted by the Bishops of Deventer and
Berne consecrated Arnold Harris Mathew in
St. Gertrude's Cathedral at Utrecht.
Hundreds of years earlier, another
Englishman, Willibrord, had brought the
Catholic faith to Utrecht and had become
the first bishop of that city. Now
England was to receive its first Old
Catholic Bishop from the Ancient See of
Utrecht. In Mathew the faith had come
full circle.

When Bishop Arnold Harris Mathew returned to England he quickly discovered
the duplicity of Fr. O'Halloran. Apart
from the congregation at Ealing, there
appeared to be no other parishes that
would identify themselves as Old Catholic.
Nor were there seventeen Roman Catholic
priests, as Fr. O'Halloran had stated.
Neither was there any evidence that there
ever had been an election. Upon discov-
ering the truth Mathew wrote to Archbishop Gul and gave him the facts and
offered to resign. It was a humble
Bishop Mathew who had to admit that he
had been deceived and who as a result became a deceiver. His offer to resign was
not accepted and the Church at Utrecht
chose to let time and circumstances determine whether they had made a mistake

in the consecration of Mathew.

Bishop Mathew took a hard look at the situation. It was one that would have discouraged anyone but the most determin- ed. Fr. O'Halloran's "supporters" were not to be found nor the 250 Roman priests who, according to the Rev. Arthur Galton in the "Fortnightly Review" were ready to break away from the tyranny of the Vatican. Neither did the thousands of Anglican priests, who were said to question their orders contact the Catholic prelate whose orders were un- questioned but who was independent of the Vatican. He had only a handful of sup- porters but he was undaunted for he reasoned that Christ also began with a very few and intended that his bishops should endure the same challenge.

He began by setting aside one of the rooms in his house at South Hampstead, as an oratory. He then ordained as deacon and priest the Rev. W. Noel Lambert who was minister of an independ- ent Congregational Church in Islington. It was the first of many instances where Congregational ministers and often their congregations with them became Old Catholic. Four months later this chapel was consecrated as St. Willibord pro- Cathedral. A half century later a dozen Congregational Churches in the United States would be served by priests and bishops in Old Catholic Orders.

Mathew on June 13, 1910 took a step that became an unfortunate precedent for hundreds of Old Catholic bishops who were

to follow him.   The Old Catholic
Churches, on the Continent, do not consecrate bishops, unless and until, the
other bishops are in agreement concerning said consecration. Yet, Archbishop
Mathew, without prior consultation and
in secret, consecrated two Roman Catholic
priests, Herbert Ignatius Beale and
Arthur William Howarth.

He argued that the consecrations were
necessary to insure the Old Catholic
succession in England.   The argument
failed to impress the continental
bishops since even in 1910 only the
English Channel separated Britain from
the continent.   Yet, the continental
bishops did not oust Mathew, they merely
sent a strongly worded protest.   But
Mathew was not to be chided and on the
twenty-ninth of December, 1910, he issued
a Declaration of Autonomy and Independ-
ence in which he cited eight reasons why
he could no longer accept direction
from Utrecht.   It should be noted that
at no time did Mathew attempt to recon-
cile these differences through discussion or negotiation.   He also continued
his relationship with the Mariavite
Church of Poland, whose bishop he had
helped consecrate at Utrecht, a few
years earlier.

The Old Catholic Church of England
was now isolated and its membership,
never large, was now less than one hundred.   Nevertheless, Archbishop Mathew
proceeded to raise four of his priests
to the office of bishop.   He was confi-
dent that each of them would go out and

as a missionary bishop win many for the
English Old Catholic Church. It was an
interesting way to attempt to build a
church from the top down, and it could
have worked if Mathew had chosen his
clergy more carefully. He did make one
fortunate choice when in 1913 he met
Rudolph Prince de Landas Berghes, an
Austrian nobleman who saw in Mathew's
church something that struck a respon-
sive chord. The Prince was a Roman
Catholic and shortly after meeting
Mathew he joined the Old Catholic Church,
received minor orders, was raised to the
priesthood, and on June 29, 1913 was
consecrated bishop. Unfortunately,
World War I broke out and the Prince because he was an enemy alien had to seek
refuge in the United States. There he
helped launch a new Old Catholic Church
under the leadership of Archbishop
Carfora which sailed through then
American skies like a comet and the
disappeared in the same manner.

In the summer of 1914 the Rev.
Frederick Samuel Willoughby came to
Bishop Mathew and asked to be received
into the Old Catholic Church. He said
that he had been forced to resign his
Anglican parish of St. John the Baptist
in Stockton on Tees because of
Protestant persecution. There is some
question as to whether these were the
correct facts but in any event, Fr.
Frederick had been asked to resign.
Arnold Harris Mathew's great weakness
was his willingness to accept everyman
at face value. He could not bring himself to investigate the backgrounds of

those who came to him and sought admission to Holy Orders. In his later years
he seemed glad to receive into the church,
clerics whose theology seemed a bit unor-
thodox. One of his priests, Fr. James
Wedgwood had asked for and was given
permission to work for the Theosophical
Society. Mathew asked that he not com-
promise his position with the Old
Catholic Church. Anson raises the
question of whether Mathew knew how
deeply involved in theosophy some of his
clergy were. I believe, there is little
doubt that Mathew knew but it seems obvious he had not considered the impli-
cations of this involvement. When he did,
it was too late, for the majority of his
clergy had embraced theosophy. On August
6, 1915 he wrote a pastoral letter and
he directed that it should be read in all
the parishes. Only one of his priests
complied with the directive. The letter
stated that any Old Catholic who belonged
to the Theosophical Society must resign.
It is noted that only two ladies actually
took the step of resigning. However,
more importantly, both Canon R. Farrer
and Canon Wedgwood resigned from Mathew's
Church, which at this time he called, The
Old Roman Catholic Church.   Most of his
clergy joined the dissidents and called
themselves Old Catholic, until they changed their name in 1917, to The Liberal
Catholic Church.

It was a bitter blow and Arnold Mathew
was getting old, tired and discouraged.
He resolved to give up the burden of his
office and sent to His Holiness Pope
Benedict XV an Act of Submission. Mathew
did not confide with anyone about this and

we shall never know his reasons or what
he expected from Rome. One thing, we
can be sure, is that he would never have
recanted his views regarding papal infallibility. Nor did Mathew ever think
that he had been a false shepherd. He
might have accepted a critical view that
would have described himself as naive and
inept, but he did believe in his vision.
He believed that England needed an autocephalous Catholic Church. Apparently,
his own view of himself was not acceptable to Rome, and Mathew found he could
not return to Rome on Pope Benedict's
terms. Yet, he did not want the burden
of continuing the work of establishing
the English Old Roman Catholic Church.
He turned over the active control of the
Church to Bishop Bernard Mary Williams,
whom he designated as the Old Catholic
Bishop of the Western District. From
May 25, 1917 until his death on the
20tn of December 1919, Arnold Harris
Mathew lived in quiet retirement. He
attended services in an Anglican Church
and from time to time ordained Anglican
clergymen who came to him in secret because they doubted the validity of their
Anglican Orders.

He was buried with Anglican rites in
the churchyard of the Anglican Church in
South Mymms. The tombstone reads as
follows:

In your charity pray for the good
estate of Arnold Harris Mathew, D. D
Bishop of the Old Catholic Church,
De Jure Earl of Landaff of Thomastown,
Co. Tipperary, who entered into rest
20th of December 1919. "Behold a
great priest who in his days pleased
God and was found just".

RUDOLPH de LANDAS BERGHES et de RACHE

1873 — 1920

The meeting of Archbishop Arnold
Harris Mathew with Prince de Landas
Berghes was historic. The two men took
an instant liking to each other for they
shared a common background and a common
faith. Prince de Landas was an Austrian
nobleman, born in Italy, and he had
traveled extensively. He was a Roman
Catholic by faith but could not accept
the view of Pius X that Arnold Harris
Mathew was a "pseudo bishop".   In fact,
the more he saw of Mathew and his church,
the more he became convinced that there
was a place, a need, and an opportunity
for a Catholic Church free of Roman
domination.

It was not long after meeting
Archbishop Mathew that Prince de Landas
became a member of the Old Catholic
Church. On November 21, 1921 he was
ordained a priest and on June 29, 1923
he was consecrated bishop. It is not
known whether Archbishop Mathew intended
that Bishop de Landas act as his auxil-
liary bishop or whether he planned to
send him to Scotland as a missionary
bishop. In any event, the war which
broke out in Europe necessitated a
change of plans. If Bishop de Landas
remained in Great Britain, he faced

internment as an enemy alien. Since he was well connected with many of the English royalty, it is thought that with the connivance of the Foreign Office he was allowed to "escape" to the United States. He arrived, significantly, on November 7, St. Willibrord's Day, 1914, to begin a short but interesting and important missionary journey in the United States.

Old Catholicism in American was at this time stronger in the United States than it was in Great Britain. The Polish National Catholic Church was growing rapidly and there were dozens of smaller groups which had been established by Archbishop Joseph Rene Vilatte. Because of the many divisions, Bishop Prince de Landas saw as his mission, the bringing together the various jurisdictions in one fold. That one fold, would, of course, be under the direction of his superior, Archbishop Arnold Mathew of England. But Bishop de Landas was unprepared for the national and jurisdictional rivalies that prevailed in America.

The Polish National Church under Bishop Francis Hodur was doing well and was very satisfied with its relationship with Utrecht. Because of this relationship they saw themselves and continue to see themselves as the sole legitimate Old Catholic Body in America. Bishop Mathew by this time had severed his relations with Utrecht and was therefore persona non grata with the Polish National Catholic Church as well.

There were many Old Catholic Churches
in the Vilatte line of succession but
few that had gathered any large following. In addition there were a few remnants of the Polish Old Catholic Church
which Utrecht had abandoned when they
decided to throw their support behind
Hodur's Polish National Catholic Church.
One of de Landas' first contacts with
American Old Catholics took place when
he met William Francis Brothers, who
was abbot of St. Dunstan's Abbey in
Waukegan, Illinois. The abbey had three
brothers and had been founded by
Monsignor Tichy. It was to be an Old
Catholic Order under the auspices of
The Protestant Episcopal Church. The
building which housed the abbey had been
provided by Bishop Charles C. Grafton of
the Episcopal Church and the Episcopal
Diocese provided funds for its support.
Bishop de Landas, with his royal background was well received by the
Episcopalians and on January 12,1915 he
participated in the consecration of
Hiram Richard Hulse, Bishop-elect of
Cuba, thus bringing the Mathew line of
succession to the Episcopal Church.
Bishop de Landas' good rapport with the
Episcopal Church was short lived. But
his friendship with William Francis
Brothers also did not last. He had
consecrated him a bishop on October 3,
1916 but Brothers was too much of a
maverick to stay long under anyone's
jurisdiction. He had successively served
as priest-abbot under Monsignor Tichy,
Archbishop Vilatte, and Bishop Grafton.
After leaving Bishop de Landas he
functioned as an independent bishop for

many years until he joined the Russian
Orthodox Church with the status of priest.
Despite this step and a very ambiguous
relationship with the Orthodox Church,
Bishop Brothers had considerable influ-
ence in the Old Catholic Movement.

But it was in Carmel Henry Carfora that
de Landas saw a future for Old Catholicism
in America. Carfora had been a priest in
the Roman Church and after a quarrel with
his bishop, he left and accepted an ap-
pointment to serve a parish in the Italian
National Church under Bishop Paolo
Miraglia-Guliotte, a bishop in the Vilatte
line. After Guliotte's retirement, Bishop
Carfora incorporated the National Catholic
Diocese in North America. In 1917 he
again changed the name of his Church to
the Old Roman Catholic Diocese and was
conditionally reconsecrated by Bishop de
Landas on October 17, 1917. No reason
was given for the reconsecration and it
began a tradition among Old Catholics in
America in which almost no jurisdcition
fully recognized the orders conferred by
another jurisdiction.

The Old Roman Catholic Diocese was made
up of parishes of almost every ethnic
group in America including Poles,Czechs,
Slovaks, Lithuanians, Ukrainians,
Italians, and Russians.   They did not
work well together and there was a con-
stant splintering of the Church.
Bishops, priests and entire parishes were
leaving regularly and occasionally a
priest would leave, only to return for a
while and leave again. This was all too
much for the Bishop Prince who was

accustomed to regularity and order. It
is said that anyone meeting Prince de
Landas realized, at once, that he was in
the presence of a royal personage merely
by the man's bearing. Most of the
priests, bishops and members of the
American Church showed little respect for
either prince or bishop and authority
within the Old Roman Catholic Diocese was
not respected. Bishop de Landas had come
to America in the hope that he might end
factionalism but he soon realized that he
had failed. In 1919 he resigned as
Metropolitan-Primate of the North American
Old Roman Catholic Church and made his
submission to the Roman See. He was received on December 22, 1919 at Saint
Patrick's Cathedral in New York City and
then retired to Villanova, Pennsylvania
were he entered the Novitiate of the
Order of St. Augustine. He died at the
monastery on November 17, 1920 at the age
of forty-seven. Although he did not
succeed in bringing together the various
Old Catholics, many of the parishes which
he and Archbishop Carfora helped establish
live on. These parishes have enlarged
and strengthened such diverse groups as
the Ukrainian Orthodox Church, the Polish
National Catholic Church, the Orthodox
Church in America, the Episcopal Church,
as well as several jurisdictions calling
themselves Old Roman Catholic and
North American Old Roman Catholic.

Archbishop Prince Ruldolph de Landas
Berghes et de Rache lies buried in the
cemetery of the Order of St. Augustine in

Villanova, Pennsylvania, and his grave is visited only occasionally by students and scholars of Old Catholic history.

Few know that here lies a "Bishop Extraordinary".

JOSEPH RENE VILATTE

1854 - 1929

It was undoubtedly Joseph Rene
Vilatte who inspired the term "Episcopi
Vagantes" which has been applied to
thousands of bishops sans roots and
established parishes. Yet, Vilatte was
a heroic figure who had a vision of an
American Catholic Church free from papal
control. He was born in Paris on
January 24, 1854 and was baptized in the
the Petite Eglise an independent
Catholic group that faded away before he
reached his maturity. His mother died
when he was still an infant and his
pious father sent him to an orphanage
in Paris run by the Brothers of the
Christian Schools.

After receiving his education, he
emigrated to Canada and was employed as
a teacher in a school near Ottawa. He
also served as catechist and often led
services in the nearby Catholic Church
when there was no priest to celebrate
mass. He remained here for two years,
when he was called up by his native
France to military service. He returned
to France, but decided that military
service was not for him and he went to

-23-

Belgium where he entered the Community
of Christian Brothers, a lay teaching
order near Namur.   He used his stay
there as a retreat during which he determined which way his life should go.
He felt the call to the priesthood and
he returned to Canada and offered his
services to Monsignor Fabre, Bishop of
Montreal.   He was sent to the College of
Saint-Laurent where he studied for three
years.   Here he met Father Charles
Chiniquy who was to have a profound influence upon his life.   Fr. Chiniquy was
thinking of leaving the Roman Church and
when he shared his thoughts with Vilatte
he succeeded in raising many doubts in
Vilatte's mind. He decided to leave
Saint-Laurent and continue his studies
at McGill University.

    In another attempt to seek direction
for his life, Vilatte went to the house
of the Clerics of St. Viator at
Bourbonnais, Illinois. While he was
there, he somehow met Father Chiniquy
again and the two of them considered the
options before Vilatte.   Father Chiniquy
knew of a large number of Belgiums who
had immigrated to Wisconsin and who had
drifted away from the Roman Church. He
suggested to Vilatte that this could be
his mission field and advised him to get
in touch with Hyacinthe Loyson, a former
Discalced Carmelite friar, who had organized the Gallican Catholic Church.
Loyson encouraged him to go to Wisconsin,
although whether he endorsed Vilatte's
idea to go an an independent Presbyterian
minister, is not known. In any event,
neither Vilatte nor the Belgiums

he was ministering to were satisfied
with this status. At Loyson's suggest-
ion he then went to the Episcopal
Bishop of Fond du Lac, J. H. Hobert
Brown and suggested that the good
bishop support him in an effort to
make the Presbyterian mission church an
Old Catholic outpost in the new world.
The bishop was aware of the number of
Belgiums who had left the church and
thought that by supporting Vilatte in
his efforts he might also promote
closer relations between the Old
Catholic Churches of Europe and the
Protestant Episcopal Church.

Bishop Brown was, of course, in a
quandary over Vilatte's insistance that
in order for his mission to succeed he
would have to go to Europe and secure
Old Catholic orders. Brown was willing to ordain him in the Episcopal
Church and was fearful that Vilatte's
action would only confirm the general
opinion concerning the invalidity of
Anglican orders. In any event Vilatte
prevailed and Bishop Brown agreed and
said he would recommend him if he would
be examined by two of the professors at
Nashotah house concerning his theological competence. His training and background insured that he would pass their
inspection and after the exam Bishop
Brown sent Bishop Herzog what can only
be described as a letter of high
praise.

With considerable difficulty
Joseph Rene Vilatte raised enough
money to travel to Switzerland where
Bishop Herzog ordained him deacon and

priest on June 6 and 7, 1885. Now
Father Vilatte began his work in earnest.
He returned to Wisconsin and opened the
mission Church of the Precious Blood in
Little Sturgeon. It was soon followed
by the opening of Blessed Sacrament
Church in Green Bay. Like so many of
the parishes founded by Old Catholics,
this mission eventually was absorbed by
another denomination. The Episcopal Church
which has on occasion befriended
American Old Catholics vilified Vilatte
and eventually gained control of the
Green Bay parish. It is today an
Episcopal parish and is often visited by
Old Catholics because of its past
association with Archbishop Vilatte.

Vilatte who is so often remembered
for his failures was quite successful
in these years in Wisconsin. Within
three years he and Father Gauthier, a
Swiss Old Catholic, served three
missions at Little Sturgeon, Green Bay
and Sycksville. During this time he
kept up an active correspondence with
the Old Catholic Bishops of Utrecht and
Deventer. During the exchange of
letters Vilatte suggested that he might
be able to function more effectively,
if he were raised to the episcopate.
When word of this reached Bishop Brown,
he wrote to Utrecht that such a step was
all right with him but if Fr. Vilatte
were raised to the episcopate the
Protestant Episcopal Church would no
longer financially support his work. The
Old Catholics of Europe were never particularly strong on missions, and the
idea that they might have to support
Vilatte's work may have been a factor in

cooling them on the idea of consecrating
him. Further, as they grew closer to the
Anglican Church, an American mission had
less appeal. Although some writers have
implied that Vilatte's erratic nature
must have figured in their thinking, the
correspondence between Vilatte and the
European bishops gives no reason for
such speculation. When the Old Catholic
Congress met in Cologne in 1890 the
bishops decided not to consecrate Father
Vilatte but gave no reasons.

If the reason for not consecrating Fr.
Vilatte was the growing closeness of the
Old Catholic Churches of Europe and the
Anglican Church, Father Joseph had a
good reason to seek the mitre. To his,
largely, Belgium parishoners, the
Protestant Episcopal Church was just what
the name implied, protestant. Father
Vilatte had been carefully, except for
accepting financial support, putting
some distance between himself and the
Episcopalians. If Utrecht were to recognize Anglican orders it would undermine
his positon. At that point he could no
longer remain with the Old Catholics of
Europe and the Protestant Episcopal
Church would no longer wish to support a
separate American Old Catholic work. One
of the purposes in supporting Vilatte in
the first place was to bring the two
communions closer together, but now it
would seem more to divide than to unify.

At this point, Fr. Vilatte's thoughts
turned to the East and he began a correspondence with Mar Julius I, the
Metropolitan of the Independent Catholic
Church of Ceylon, Goa, and India. The

Church, although consisting of only about
5,000 Catholics of the Latin Rite, was in
communion with the Jacobite Patriarch of
Antioch and had unquestioned valid orders.
Further this Patriarch had consecrated
Julius Ferrette as Bishop of Iona in 1866
and he was presumably seeking ways to extend the influence of his small communion
to the West. When both Bishop Alvarez
(Mar Julius I) and his Patriarch responded favorably, Father Joseph felt he knew
what had to be done.

Although, he was often painted as
ambitious it seemed clear that either his
struggling Wisconsin parishes would ultimately have to merge with the Episcopal
Church or upon Fr. Vilatte's death would
pass out of existence. Although his
flock was small, they held a synod and
elected him bishop and the Dyckesville
parish raised $225.00 for his passage to
India. Bishop Grafton upon hearing the
news reacted even more violently than he
had to the idea of Vilatte being consecrated in Utrecht. He wrote a strong
letter of protest to the Patriarch and to
Bishop Alvarez, but it was seen, at least,
by Mar Julius, as a spiteful letter intended to pay off an old grudge. Father
Joseph Rene Vilatte was raised to the
episcopate in Ceylon on May 29, 1892.

It was probably the most controversial
consecration in modern times. Peter
Anson suggested that Vilatte went to
Ceylon lest Alvarez discover how few
Americans desired to separate themselves
from Rome. But it cannot be said that
the Church authorities in Antioch and
India did not have sufficient opportunity

or time to acquaint themselves with the
facts in the case. Bishop Grafton and
others did everything possible to discredit Vilatte. The mere fact that the
petition to consecrate was only signed
by one clergyman would have been sufficient to indicate to everyone that
Fr. Joseph's following was small. Much
has been made of the fact that the supporters of Vilatte were few and uned-
ucated. The poverty of many Old
Catholic bishops has been stressed in
such a way as to imply that holy poverty
is to be reserved only for the lower
clergy.

The newly consecrated bishop returned to a very small indigenous church.
The chapel of St. Louis at Green Bay
was raised to the status of a pro-
cathedral and two other parishes remained in his jurisdiction, St. Joseph's,
Walhain, and St. Mary's at Duval. With
few resources, few clergy, and a few
missionary minded laymen, Vilatte worked
indefatigably to build a strong American
Catholic Church. For a short while he
published "The Old Catholic" but since
he had to do all the writing himself and
it did not receive a great deal of support, he turned his energy to other concerns. He did find time to publish a
small prayer book and catechism.

In all Vilatte spent five years in
Wisconsin after his consecration. Pro-
gress was slow and the Church never
numbered more than five hundred souls.
He felt it was time for him to move to
other, more promising, mission fields. He

appointed Fr. Gauthier as pastor of the
three small parishes and expected that
he would be able to continue the work.
The mission did not grow under Father
Gauthier's ministry and the two priests
who succeeded him proved to be incapable
shepherds. In time the parishes drifted
either into the Protestant Episcopal
Church or disbanded.

At this point in his career Bishop
Vilatte was not certain concerning his
mission. For a brief while he thought he
might build his American Old Catholic
Church among the large number of Poles
who immigrated to this country. He
consecrated Father Stephen Kaminski on
March 21, 1898 and designated him as his
Assistant Bishop. Although Bishop
Kaminski served a small congregation in
Buffalo, New York until his death in
1911, he never succeeded in bringing
many of his countrymen into The
American Old Catholic Church.

In the last years of his life,
Archbishop Joseph Vilatte would make two
permanent contributions to Catholic life.
He would bring Holy Orders to two religious bodies which owed him nothing
for their existence. The first was the
Order of St. Benedict which had a
monastery in a remote part of Wales. The
monks who built Llanthony knew nothing
of Vilatte's existence until he appeared
one day at their monastery gates.

The African Orthodox Church grew out
of the movement founded by Marcus Garvey,
a West Indian, who encouraged blacks in

America to take pride in their race and
raise themselves up by tugging on their
own bootstraps.

What both of these disparate groups
needed from Vilatte were valid Catholic
Orders. The Monks of Llanthony were
led by "Father" Ignatius, who like
Vilatte, had a vision but unlike Vilatte
he was able to accomplish what he set
out to do. He was born Joseph
Leycester Lyne on November 23, 1837
and from childhood on sought to live a
religious life. It is reported by one
of his biographers that his troubles in
school were due not to mischievous be-
havior but by being better than his
teachers through normal for a child. His
approach to faith was anti-intellectual
and as a result when he studied for Holy
Orders he did poorly in such subjects as
theology, philosophy, and Biblical criticism. He knew the Bible and liturgics,
but these have more to do with the heart
than the mind. At least, as Joseph Lyne
approached these two subjects.

He studied for the priesthood at
Trinity College, Glenamond and was ordained a deacon on December 23, 1860.
His work at the college was so poor
that it was decided that he would have
to remain a deacon for three years before he could seek ordination to the
priesthood. During these three years it
was thought that he would study and pre-
pare himself to be a priest. He was
forbidden to preach until he was ordained a priest.

His religious orientation was decided-
ly high church. He believed with all his
heart that the Anglican Church was a true
Catholic Church and it was his calling to
lead people in the practice of the
Catholic faith. He also felt the call to
the monastic life. This presented a ser-
ious problem since the Anglican Church
together with the English government had
managed to suppress the monasteries and
cloisters throughout the land.   To live
a monastic life in the Anglican Church at
that time first required that a monastic
order and a monastery be established.

Neither were there many Anglo Catholic
parishes where a young seminarian could
receive further training, particularly in
the area of practical theology. However,
he did find The Rev. George Rundle Prynne
of St. Peter's, Plymouth. Fr. Praynne
was a well known Tractarian priest, who
already had a curate and whose parish
could hardly afford a second. Fortunately,
Lyne had a small legacy which enabled him
to serve St. Peters without pay. While
serving St. Peters the young deacon devoted much of his time and energy to re-
cruiting young men interested in the
monastic life. Although it did not
differ much from a number of other
English male communities living under
discipline, he organized the "Society of
the Love of Jesus". At this time he became "Brother" Joseph and served the
small group as its Superior. Perhaps one
reason why he decided to serve St.
Peter's in Plymouth was the fact that a
women's order calling itself St.

Dunstan's Abbey was nearby.   At any
rate, he went to St. Dunstan's and met
with its Abbess, Mother Lydia.   The
meeting did much to strengthen his de-
termination to found a monastic order
based on the Rule of St. Benedict.   He
also found a sponsor who could obtain
financial support for the new community.
Before Mother Lydia was willing to give
her support, she asked that he visit Dr.
E. B. Pusey.   After the meeting, Dr.
Pusey and Mother Lydia decided to support the young deacon and offered him
the use of a house belonging to Mother
Lydia.   Unfortunately, no sooner did
Brother Joseph and two of his followers
move in, he was stricken with typhoid
fever and the founding of a Benedictine
Order was postponed.

Brother Joseph was taken by his
family to Belgium to convalesce.   His
father hoped he would give up any ideas
of monastic vocation, but upon his return
he immediately started to gather recruits
for the Monastic Order of St. Benedict.
He worked in many English communities and
endured persecution from the Church of
England and from Protestants outside of
the established Church.   Finally, almost
in desperation, he brought his followers
to a remote area of Wales.   It was close
to the site of a long closed abbey and
they called their abbey, the New
Llantony Abbey of Our Ladye and St.
Dunstan in the Valley of Weyas".   In
1870 they purchased 34 acres of land
that were unsuited for anything but
what it was intended for, "a retreat
from the world."   Here the brothers

built their abbey, complete with a beau-
tiful Abbey Church. To support it
Joseph Lyne, now "Father" Ignatius had
to out and preach in as many Anglo
Catholic parishes as he could find. The
funds which he raised were vital for the
continuation of the community.

Because the community was so remote,
it was only occasionally that a sympa-
thetic Anglo Catholic priest would come
by and provide the Blessed Sacrament for
the monks. For a group that considered
itself catholic, this was highly unsatis-
factory, but "Father" Ignatius had never
been able to interest a priest in joining the order. Yet, the monks were well
known, since they were modern pioneers
for the monastic movement in the Anglican
Church. Even though they did not have
the approval of any Anglican authority
and were led by "Father" Ignatius, who
by going ahead and preaching without
episcopal authority had placed himself
outside of the Church, most Tractarian
sympathisers viewed the monks as their
own. The monks at Llanthony were regarded even by their most ardent supporters as "strange" but they were a challenge to the Established Church to provide what many high churchmen felt was a
need, a monastery where those who felt
called to the contemplative life could
go and offer needed prayers for the
church.

Somehow news of their plight reached
Bishop Vilatte while he was in Buffalo
in 1898 and he resolved to go to
Llanthony and offer them his services.

He was the first bishop to come to the
community since its founding in 1870 and
he was welcomed with great joy. What he
proposed to do was to provide them with a
priest. He would ordain "Father"
Ignatius, and several other brothers so
that the community would not be without
a priest when Father Ignatius was away
on his fund raising trips. After the
ordinations, Bishop Vilatte blessed
Ignatius as Abbot. It all seems so
simple and straightforward but it creat-
ed an unseemly stir in the Anglican
Church. Forgotten was the fact that
these monks had pioneered and held out
the idea of Anglican cloisters for many
years. Also forgotten was the fact that
Ignatius was, indeed, the abbot, and he
also functioned as "priest" to the monks.
He did not, of course, offer the Mass or
the Sacrament of Confession, but in every
other respect he was shepherd and priest.
No bishop of the Anglican Church appeared either to regularize this situation or
to provide a priest for the abbey. When
the monks turned to the only bishop who
offered to provide priests for the abbey,
they were widely critized. Peter Anson
would later say, "All that was gained by
these highly irregular ordinations was
that Abbot Ignatius and his monks became
schismatics in the eye of Anglo Catholics,
instead of holy eccentrics who deserved
pity and even admiration." It is true
that the step cut off much of the support
which the Abbey at Llanthony had been get-
ing from Anglican admirers and parishes.
But now for the first time they could
celebrate daily Mass and lead a full sacramental life. The motives of Bishop

Vilatte have been questioned, but none
can question that the ordinations en-
riched the monastery.

Vilatte's role in the founding of the
African Orthodox Church was in many ways
similar. It, like the ordinations at
Llanthony, brought nothing to Bishop
Vilatte's jurisdiction but he brought
great benefit to the African Orthodox
Church. In the early part of the
twentieth century there were many black
people who were members of the Protestant
Episcopal Church. Large numbers of these
lived in the West Indies and they responded to the leadership of Marcus Garvey, a
Jamaican, who founded the Universal
Negro Improvement Association. Garvey
preached black pride and urged his fellow Negroes to strive to improve their
lot by relying on their own resources,
skills, and leadership. It was not long
before the black Episcopalians felt that
their needs would be better served by a
black bishop. The Episcopal Church had a
number of black priests, but it did not
respond to the plea for a bishop of color.
Surely there were any number of quali-
fied black candidates and no good reason
why one of them should not be consecrated
bishop, a number of black Episcopalians
withdrew and formed the African Orthodox
Church. They elected one of their number,
Father George Alexander McGuire to be
their bishop.   Father McGuire was close-
ly associated with Marcus Garvey and had
formerly been an Episcopal missionary in
the West Indies.

But like the monks at Llanthony, no

one heeded their cry for help when they
sought a consecrator for their newly
elected bishop. They had appealed to
the Russian Orthodox hierarchy but were
refused when it was apparent that they
had no greater desire to be ruled by
the Russian Orthodox hierarchy than by
the Anglican hierarchy. What they
wanted was to be free to direct the des-
tiny of their own church without outside interference. On September 18,
1921 at the Church of Our Lady of Good
Death in New York City, George
Alexander McGuire was consecrated bishop
by the Most Rev. Joseph Rene Vilatte.
Vilatte asked nothing in return, but
felt he was performing a service for an
entire race of people. The African
Orthodox Church has provided the
Sacraments of the Church for thousands
of blacks who sought a truly Catholic
and Sacramental Church in which they
could have full participation

It was the last important act in the
life of Bishop Vilatte and he was growing old and tired. He had traveled
widely and he had more failures than
successes in his life and he felt very
much alone. He had no close associates
and therefore we do not know what
reasons he had to seek reconciliation
with Rome. In any event, he went to live
at the Abbey of Pon-Colbert, a
Cistercian Abbey near Versailles. Here
he lived until his death on July 8,
1929 when a requiem Mass was celebrated
as for a layman and thus the man who

would rival the Pope was buried without
honors.   But if Vilatte did nothing
more than consecrate George McGuire,
who proved to be a truly great church-
man, he would deserve the title of
Bishop Extrordinary.

CARMEL HENRY CARFORA

1878 - 1958

Born in Naples, Italy on August 27, 1878 Carmel Henry Carfora was guided into the priesthood from a very early age. His parents, Ferdinand and Angela Carfora wanted their son to become a priest and encouraged him until at the age of seventeen he entered the Order of Friars Minor. When he was twenty three he was ordained to the priesthood. He was a good student and he was encouraged by the Church to study, first in the University of Naples where he earned his Doctorate in Philosophy and later in the Theological Institute of Naples where he earned a Doctorate of Sacred Theology. Believing him well prepared the Church sent him to the United States to minister to the Italian immigrants.

For two years he worked in various Roman Catholic parishes from New York to West Virginia. The reasons are lost in history but Fr. Carfora incurred the wrath of Bishop Falconion, the Apostolic Delegate to the United States. Fr. Carfora was outspoken, in a time when

priests were supposed to give unquestioned obedience, so it is easy to believe he could have displeased his
superiors. What he did next was an even
greater departure from Roman tradition.
He left the Roman Church to open an independent Catholic mission. It prospered
in spite of heavy opposition from the
Roman Church. In addition to serving as
pastor of St. Rocchus Italian National
Catholic Church he managed to serve two
other small mission parishes.

It was inevitable that Fr. Carfora
would soon cross paths with Bishop
Paolo Miraglia-Guliotti, who headed the
Italian National Episcopal Church.
Bishop Guliotti was consecrated by
Archbishop Joseph Vilatte and had been
one of Vilatte's suffragan bishops.
They cooperated in ministering to
Italian Americans and in 1911 Bishop
Guliotti consecrated Carmel Henry
Carfora. Yet the new bishop did not
serve in the Italian Episcopal Church
but organized in Ohio, the National
Catholic Diocese in North America. In
the next few years Carfora traveled
thoughout the East and Mid-West and began to feel that he had a mission
larger than the Italian-American community.

Another fortuitous meeting took place
in 1916. This time he crossed paths
with Bishop Prince de Landas Berghes et
de Rache, who represented Arbishop
Arnold Harris Mathew of the Old Roman
Catholic Church of England. Shortly
after their meeting Bishop de Landas
joined with Carfora after reconsecrating

him on October 4 of that year. No
reasons for the reconsecration have
ever been given. It may simply be that
the Old Catholics in America were doing
as their Orthodox brethren, recognizing
only those consecrations which were
made by their own particular jurisdiction. It is an unfortunate and strange
departure from Western Catholic tradition. But be that as it may, the
coming together of Bishop de Landas and
Bishop Carfora was a new beginning for
Old Catholicism in America.

Bishop Carfora selected Chicago as
his See City and it was a wise choice.
Chicago, more than any American city,
except New York, was a city of ethnic
neighborhoods. Bishop Carfora set
about finding priests in each of these
neighborhoods and began to gather
ethnic parishes. It was a formula
that worked so well that he was soon
sending missionaries to every American
city that had significant ethnic
neighborhoods. It was not long before
he had raised to bishop a priest for
each of the many ethnic groups that
become part of the Old Roman Catholic
Church. It is significant that there
were few parishes of either Irish or
German background. The reason is
obvious. The Roman Church in the
United States, at this time, had as
its bishops and priests, men from
either Irish or German background. It
was a fact resented by other ethnics
and they found it seasy to leave the
church to follow a bishop from their
own ethnic group. Sometimes, of course,

ethnicity worked against Bishop Carfora
and the North American Old Roman
Catholic Church. His bishop in
Manchester, New Hampshire was Roman W.
Slocinski, who had built a very solid
parish in the Polish community in that
city. He found it difficult to get
along with his Italian superior. In
time this parish would find its way into
the Polish National Catholic Church as
would many other Polish parishes in
Carfora's jurisdiction. He built a large
following among the Lithuanians and the
Ukrainians. For each group he consecrated bishops, namely Sigismund K. Vipartas
for the Lithuanians and Basil Drapak for
the Ukrainians.. The one thing all
these ethnic groups had in common was
that they tended to be Poles, Ukrainians
or Lithuanians first, and Catholics
second. Since ethnic reasons played so
large a part in their joining the North
American Old Roman Catholic Church in
the first place, it was only natural
that this would be the very force that
would cause them to leave the NAORCC and
form a national church for their own
people.

Even during Bishop Carfora's lifetime many of these ethnic parishes left
and took with them a substantial number
of buildings which had been dedicated
by Archbishop Carfora. Some have in-
scriptions in their cornerstones design-
ating the building as being North
American Old Roman Catholic but now are
Ukrainian, Polish, or a church of some
other ethnic group. Yet, at the beginning, Carfora seemed to cut a wide
swath. Thousands came and joined the

new Church. Most were dissatisfied
Roman Catholics, although a significant
number of Episcopalians were to be
counted among his converts. Among the
latter were many clergymen who had
doubts about Anglican orders.

Although the Church was usually
classified as Old Catholic, it was an
inaccurate label for many reasons.
First of all, Archbishop Carfora regarded himself as infallible, and the
liturgy and practices of the church
were quite consistent with its title
of Old Roman Catholic. The remnants
which remain today argue that Utrecht
left the main stream of non-papal
Catholicism when it recognized
Anglican orders. In spite of, or perhaps, because of, the fact that
Carfora considered himself to be infallible the Church was beset by
many internal problems. Of course,
the type of clergy it attracted did
not help. Most of the clergymen were
dissatisfied Roman Catholics or
Anglicans and, if they had problems in
their former churches, they seemed to
have brought them into the new. Even
as they quarreled with their former
bishops, so they now quarreled with
Archbishop Carfora. I have known
several priests who served under him
who said he was a very kindly gentleman,
yet he deposed priests and bishops at
an alarming rate. Most of those deposed went off to start new jurisdictions
of their own taking members and
property with them.

Carfora had not forgotten Bishop de
Landas' vision of a united American
independent Catholic Church. For a
while, he joined with Archbishop
Frederick Ebenezer Lloyd and the
American Catholic Church under the title
of "The Holy Catholic Church in America".
The new body was formed in 1925 and in
less than a year they went their
separate ways. The desire for unity,
which by itself was a legitimate and
noble goal, would become a destructive
force in Old Roman Catholicism and in
Old Catholicism. Each attempt at unity
would only exacerbate their differences.
As the movement declined and there were
fewer and fewer congregations to unite,
the law of diminishing returns set in.
In eccleasiastical circles it is known
that the smaller the church body the
more difficult it is to unite it with
other church bodies. Much of the time
and effort that should have gone into
the care and feeding of the flock was
devoted to many fruitless efforts to
create a united independent Catholic
Church for America.

What effort Archbishop Carfora
devoted to outreach tended in the direction of searching out new ethnic groups
that desired or according to Carfora
should desire a Catholic Church to call
their own.   He devoted a great deal of
effort in 1926 to extend the North
American Old Roman Catholic Church to
Mexico. He consecrated Jose Joachin
Perez y Budar on October 17, 1926 for
the Iglesia Ortodoxa Catolica Mexicana.

This was a group which had made a promising start in Mexico but no sooner did
they get a bishop; they began to decline.
Carfora never understood and neither did
his successors that parishes could be
gathered under priests,who were separated from Rome, but when they became
bishops, or bishops appeared on the
scene many of the Roman Catholics who
worshipped in those parishes became
acutely aware of their separation from
Rome and hastily returned to the Mother
Church. Catholics are comfortable with
their priests, even those who have left
Rome, but they are seldom comfortable
with their bishops and certainly not
bishops outside of the Roman Church.
Often Carfora would send a priest into a
neighborhood and a parish would be formed. The priest was often well received
and became liked by the people. When
the nearby Roman priest would criti-
cize or even warn them against the new
priest they would usually continue to
support the priest and the Old Roman
Catholic parish they had come to love.
Once begun these parishes often grew at
a steady pace. However, often the
priest demanded a mitre from Carfora or
was given one because this was the manner in which Carfora rewarded those who
had been successful. Frequently, it had
a stulifying effect upon parish growth
and just as frequently these new bishops
tended to break away and create new
jurisdictions.

The Mexican Catholic Church never
became very large or significant in

Mexico. Today there are a few remnant parishes in many places in Mexico but they are disorganized, poor and disunited. Los Angeles has one parish, St. Augustine's which was established in 1908 and is served by Bishop Emile Rodrigues y Fairfield. It is one of the oldest parishes once connected with the Church founded by Bishop Carfora that has not been swallowed by one of the larger Churches.

It is difficult to determine how many members the North American Old Roman Catholic Church had in any one year. Jonathan Trela cites a figure of 114,793 souls in 1926. It may have been larger a decade earlier for in 1922 Carfora had the synod of the Church elect him as Supreme Head of all Old Roman Catholic Churches in America and he assumed the title of "The Most Illustrious Lord, the Supreme Primate of the North American Old Catholoic Church" and declared that "All doctrinal laws or new articles of faith shall be considered final when he (i.e. Carfora) speaks ex cathedra" This did not set well with many and the exodus began to accelerate.

Unfortunately as one bishop after another left, Carfora would replace them by consecrating new bishops. It proved to be a very poor solution. For example, on September 21, 1926 he consecrated Charles Alphonse Blanchard as Bishop of Portland, Oregon. In less than a year Bishop Blanchard left Carfora to begin yet another independent Catholic Church.

In 1931 he became aware of the fact that
more of his prelates and members were
outside of his jurisdiction than he had
within it. He consecrated James
Christian Crummey and directed him to
form one of the first of the "umbrella"
churches, i.e. the Universal Episcopal
Communion" which was suppossed to bring
the various separated churches into some
kind of body that would be in communion
with the NAORCC. He achieved a measure
of success before he himself broke with
Carfora and the organization fell apart
with the death of Crummy in 1949.

When Bishop Carmel Henry Carfora died
on January 11, 1958, he did not leave
behind him a strong centralized church
organization. What followed was a
further splintering of his already
small jurisdiction and the claims of, at
least, six bishops to be his one and
only legitimate successor. But on the
positive side it must be granted that
Bishop Carfora brought back into the
Church thousands of ethnics who had
been dissatisfied and felt that their
own concerns and ethnic values had been
ignored. Through Carfora's work they
ultimately found themselves in the
various national churches: Ukrainian,
Polish, Lithuania, etc. Carfora never
thought of his church as a vestibule
church but for thousands it was just
that. It is no small accomplishment for
Carfora lived in an America that was
divided into small ethnic neighborhoods
and each was struggling for a place in
the sun. The tendency of many was to
leave many Old World customs and values
behind. Thousands had left the church

and only returned when they saw it not
only as a means of salvation for their
souls, but saw it as preserving their
language and those values of the Old
World which had value in the new.

   Carfora has been described as a kindly, considerate and dedicated individual.
Many, today, are proud to claim that the
they are in Carfora's line of succession
and a few claim to be his "legitimate"
successor.   A few even have a trunk
full of documents to substantiate their
claims, but let me suggest a better and
more accurate test.   A rule of the Church
is that the church is where the bishop
is.   Would it not be equally true, that
where there are parishes, established by
Carfora, that acknowledge a particular
bishop as head of the North American Old
Roman Catholic Church that he is the
church's bishop?   If the bishop validates
the church than the church, in turn,
validates the bishop.

AFTIMIOS OFIESH

1880 - 1971

The story of Aftimios Ofiesh is the
story of a man of great dedication, who
was given an impossible task, but whose
unflagging courage enabled him to keep
before the American Orthodox a great and
noble vision. He believed that
America's millions of Orthdox Christians
could be brought together into one
independent American Orthodox Church. In
his lifetime, he did not succeed but his
accomplishments were many. Because of
his life and work, every ethnic Orthodox
Church in America has had to come to
grips with the question of language and
unity.

He was born, Abdullah Ofiesh, on
October 22, 1880 in Bikfaya, Lebanon,
the sixth child of Father Gabriel
Ofiesh and his wife, Badrah. He very
early decided he would seek Holy Orders
and he was entered into the theological
seminary in Beirut. After his gradu-
ation, he became a deacon, taking the
name Aftimios and he served on the
staff of Bishop Gabriel in Beirut. He
was an able administrator and was much
interested in promoting better relations between Moslems and Christians.
He was ordained a priest in 1902 and

-49-

served the bishop's office until 1905 when he expressed a desire to serve in America and was given permission to go to New York where he would serve under Bishop Raphael Hawaweeny, the Bishop of Brooklyn.

The Diocese of Brooklyn was a Syrian diocese under the jurisdiction of the Russian Orthodox Church. The Russian Church, which was first in America, attempted to minister to all the Orthodox, regardless of national origin. Bishop Raphael recognized, at once, the abilities of his new priest and appointed him Dean of St. Nicholas Cathedral in Brooklyn. Fr. Aftimios was soon seen as the unusual person that he was. Sent on a trip throughout the diocese to raise much needed money, he visited a needy widow in Pittsburgh and gave her the rest of his expense money. He had to borrow from a traveling companion in order to return home. Apart from that minor setback the trip was a success.

Because he had been successful in resolving problems that had arisen in St. Nicholas Church in Montreal, he was appointed as its pastor. He spent eleven years there and raised sufficient money to build a new and larger church. However, ethnic rivalries caused a schism in the parish and when one faction withdrew the parish was renamed St. George Syrian Orthodox Church. Throughout America, ethnic loyalties were threatening the unity of the Russian Orthodox Church. Bishop Raphael, who felt that his true spiritual home was Antioch, was calling the Arab congre-

gations to come out of the Russian
Church. By 1924 he could claim the loy-
alty of 24 parishes and most of them had
formerly been a part of the Russian
Orthodox Church. Upon the death of
Bishop Raphael an attempt was made to
bring back the dissident churches
through the cooperative efforts of the
Syrian and Russian Church authorities.
Metropolitan Germanos thought union
might be possible if he could persuade
the Patriarch of Antioch to send a
bishop to America to help him consecrate
Father Aftimios to be bishop to the
Syrians in America. Part of the plan
would be for Fr. Aftimios to renounce
his Russian superior. Aftimios refused.

Next the Russians decided that
Aftimios was the man to succeed Bishop
Raphael and they consecrated him on
May 13, 1917 at St. Nicholas Russian
Orthodox Cathedral in New York City.
The new bishop, although facing many
problems, went immediately to work to
rebuild the diocese. He organized
Bible study groups and laid the foun-
dation for training church choirs and
Sunday School teachers. In 1923 he or-
ganized the first Orthodox orphanage in
America, which was open to any child of
Arab parentage, regardless of religious
affiliation. In spite of his success
in office, he continued to be troubled
by the ethnic disputes which rocked not
only his diocese but the entire
Orthodox Church in America. It wasn't
until February 2, 1927 that his real
mission began. At this time
Metropolitan Platon charged Archbishop

Aftimios with the task of providing
America with a distinctly American
Orthodox Church. Not only was the plan
supported by the Metropolitan but he had
the support of the ruling bishops of the
Russian Orthodox Metropolia.

The plan to organize the Holy Eastern
Orthodox Catholic and Apostolic Church
in North America was to transfer the
parishes of the Diocese of Brooklyn to
the new jurisdiction. A parish wishing
to join the new Church would petition
Archbihop Aftimios for a release from
his authority as Bishop of Brooklyn and
then would request the President of the
Holy Synod of the new body to take authority over the parish. Aftimios held a
dual role which should have paved the
way towards making his dream a reality.
The new Church would be free from all
control, English would be the liturgical
language, and it would include Orthodox
from every ethnic background. A new
publication, the "Orthodox Catholic
Review" was sponsored and it appeared in
the spring and summer of 1927 It con-
tained articles on faith and traditions
and was directed towards non-Orthodox
Americans who might be interested in
exploring Orthodoxy.

Opposition quickly came from almost
every conceivable quarter. The different Orthodox jurisdictions all
blasted the new Church. The Protestant
Episcopal Church, as might be expected,
also joined in with the chorus of criticism. The Episcopalians saw themselves
as the English language alternative to

Orthodoxy and therefore a new Orthodox
Church using English and claiming to be
an "American" Church was seen as a
threat. More damaging was the denun-
ciation by the Russian Bishops in exile
at Karlovsty, Yugoslavia who took the
position that the formation of the new
Church was a violation of canon law.

The criticism did undercut the support for the new church. Few of the
parishes in the Diocese of Brooklyn
elected to join the new church, but
adopted a wait and see policy. It did
not take long for Metropolitan Platon
and the Russian Orthodox Metropolia to
withdraw their support and on July 15,
1929 Archbishop Aftimios and his supporters voted to go it alone. Although it was to be autocephalous, the
new church vowed "to preserve at all
times its brotherly and filial relationship to the Orthodox Church of Russia",
and, of course, to look for direction
from the Patriarchate of Moscow and All
Russia.

It seemed to be an idea whose time
had come, and the new "Orthodox Catholic
Review" began to publish articles which
were controversial but today would hardly raise an eyebrow. In the "Review"
Ofiesh argued for an American Church
that would be free from foreign control
and the attempt to preserve Old World
culture and customs in America.   In
one issue of the "Review" he said,
"More than half the Orthodox in America
today are the American reared and edu-
cated children of the Orthodox immigrants. These young people and their

children are to be the Orthodox of
America tomorrow. They know little and
care less about the racial and national
prejudices and jurisdictional quarrels of
Europe. Those things are very foreign
and strange to their American training
and interests. A Church that bases its
claim to their membership and allegiance
on the language, nationality, or racial
prejudices of their grandfathers will
mean nothing to them. They rightly de-
mand a Church that is concerned primar-
ily with their own conditions and problems in America rather than with the
politics of the Balkans, Greece, Russia,
or Syria. That an American Church should
include all those nationalities on the
common basis of their Orthodoxy and
American residence is natural and fit-
ting."

Although, only a few responded by be-
coming part of an American Orthodox
Church his vision lives on. First, there
are those churches whose bishops' orders
are in the Ofiesh lineage. THE OLD
CATHOLIC SOURCEBOOK lists twenty of them,
including the Eastern Orthodox Catholic
Church in America, Christ Catholic Church,
and The Holy Orthodox Church, American
Jurisdiction. While these twenty jurisdictions only number a few thousands,
their existence puts pressure on the
Canonical Orthodox Churches to
Americanize. A few have introduced
English as the principal liturgical language and have made provision for
Western Rite vicariates.

After Metropolitan Platon withdrew his
support, Archbishop Ofiesh and the

American Orthodox Church became more
isolated. During its period of isola-
tion, both the Church and the Archbishop became even more Americanized.
Perhaps because he regarded many of the
Orthodox canons better suited for different times and different cultures, he
ignored the Canon that a bishop may not
marry and in 1933 he married. He was
quickly deposed because not even his
closest followers were ready for this
departure from Orthodox tradition. When
he died in 1971 there were few followers
left to mourn. Interestingly, among the
twenty or more jurisdictions that claim
the Ofiesh lineage about half are
ruled by married bishops. None of the
existing churches in that lineage use
any other language than English in the
Liturgy, and three quarters of them are
Western Rite. Although the main line
Orthodox Churches are organized along
ethnic lines, the wall of separation between them is gradually crumbling and
here and there when new Orthodox
parishes are organized they more often
than not are made up of Orthodox from
various ethnic backgrounds. Almost
everywhere it is recognized that the
dream of Aftimious Ofiesh, Bishop
Extraordinary, will someday be realized
as the various Orthodox Churches come
closer together in unity.

Bibliography

Anson, Peter F.   "Bishops at Large",
                         New York, October
                         House Inc. 1964,
                         593 pp

Calder-Marshall,   "The Enthusiast",
Arthur   London: Faber &
                         Faber, 1962, 304 pp

Holman, John E.   "The Old Catholic
                         Church"
                         Milwaukee, WI:
                         Port Royal Press,
                         1977, 121 pp

Moss, C. B.   "The Old Catholic
                         Movement"
                         New York:
                         Morehouse-Barlow
                         1964, 2nd edition
                         Episcopal Book Club,
                         1977, 368 pp

Pruter, Karl   "A History of the
                         Old Catholic
                         Church"
                         Scottsdale,
                         St. Willibrord's
                         1973,   76 pp

Pruter, Karl &   "The Old Catholic
J. Gordon Melton   Sourcebook"
                         New York: Garland
                         Publishing, 1983,
                         254 pp

Schultz, Paul   "A History of the
                       Apostolic Succession
                       of Archbishop Emile
                       F. Rodrigues-
                       Fairfield From the
                       Mexican National
                       Catholic Church
                       Iglesia Ortodoxa
                       Catolica Apostolica
                       Mexicana" second
                       edition
                       Glendale, CA: Dr.
                       Paul Schultz, 1983,
                       43 pp

Tarsar, C. J. ed.   "Orthodox America
                       1794-1976"
                       New York, The
                       Orthodox Church in
                       America,   1975,
                       351 pp

Trela, Jonathan   "A History of the
                       North American Old
                       Roman Catholic
                       Church"
                       Scranton, PA:
                       Jonathan Trela,
                       1979,   124 pp

magazines:

Morris, John W.   "The Episcopate of
                       Aftimios Ofiesh"
                       THE WORD (Feb pp 5-9
                       Mar pp 5-10 1981)

www.ingramcontent.com/pod-product-compliance
Lightning Source LLC
Chambersburg PA
CBHW031528040426

42445CB00009B/442